THE *not so* RETIRING COOK

100 Celebrity Recipes
for the Over 60's

GRUB STREET · LONDON

Published by Grub Street, The Basement,
10 Chivalry Road, London SW11 1HT

A catalogue record of this book is available from
the British Library.

ISBN 0 948817 66 6

Edited by Lady Georgina Coleridge and
Anne Dolamore

Co-ordinator Jennifer Finegold (in loving memory
of Kitty and David Grant)

Sponsored by 🌸 **BARCLAYS**

Photographs by Tim Imrie

Food preparation and styling by Anne Dolamore

Illustrations by Madeleine David

Design by Graeme Andrew

Typesetting by BMD Graphics, Hemel Hempstead

Printed and bound by Biddles Ltd, Guildford and
King's Lynn

CONTENTS

RECIPES

SPONSOR'S MESSAGE

Brian
Carr

As supporters of Elderly Accommodation Counsel, we are particularly pleased to sponsor this fascinating publication – 'The Not So Retiring Cook' in time to mark the occasion of the EC European Year of the Elderly in 1993.

The bank's association with Elderly Accommodation Counsel began six years ago when we became the first company to subscribe to their special service for company pensioners. Since then, many of our pensioners around the country have benefited from the charity's information, advice and counselling services.

Barclays funds a substantial and wide ranging programme of community activities which focuses on charitable donations and sponsorships, secondment of staff, employment initiatives as well as support for environment projects and the arts. One of our specific charitable objectives is to encourage elderly people to live active, fulfilled lives to as great an age as possible and we have no doubt that this cookery book will bring great enjoyment to many.

Some eminent people from varied walks of life have contributed to this collection of recipes and we wish the book and Elderly Accommodation Counsel every success for the future.

Brian Carr
Head of Barclays Community Enterprise
Barclays Bank PLC

EAC AT WORK

The two charities behind this book are both young in years and heart but they are dedicated to the welfare of those over 60.

Elderly Accommodation Counsel (EAC) was established by Michael and Angela Farnell in 1985 because they had experienced great difficulties trying to find the right accommodation for elderly relatives in their later years. The Farnells found it a problem to get information of any kind and realised that it was probably the same for everyone in their situation.

This Charity, which now deals with thousands of enquiries a year, holds on computer information on all the various accommodation options available for people over 60 who feel the need to move from their present home. This register covers sheltered housing for rent and for sale; sheltered accommodation, being a bed sitting room with some meals provided, but maintaining, within reason, the independence of the individual; residential care; nursing homes and lastly terminal hospices.

EAC can also offer advice and counsel on State benefits for those going into care and on possible sources of 'top up' funding for those who are unable to manage from their own resources.

Finally, EAC carries out major research studies into existing accommodation for elderly people; the results of these studies are of benefit, not only to those who are responsible for planning and building future housing and homes for the elderly, but also for expanding the Charity's own data base.

The Association of Friends of Elderly Accommodation Counsel was founded only two years ago to act as the interface between EAC, those who use the Charity's services, and those who provide the accommodation and care to look after the elderly. Its job is to promote EAC, help to educate the public and the authorities who cater for the needs of our growing elderly population and last but not least to fund-raise for EAC.

Anyone, individuals, companies, young or old can become a member of the 'Friends' and by supporting the Charity help us to achieve our objective – a better quality of life for everyone over 60.

For further information about either Charity you should write to:

**Angela Farnell,
EAC, 46A Chiswick High Road,
London W4 1SZ.**

LIST OF CONTRIBUTORS

The publishers and the Friends of Elderly Accommodation Counsel would like to thank the following contributors for their favourite recipes, without which this book would not have been possible.

Audrey Slaughter
The Baroness Sharples
Terence Cuneo
Lady Grade
Lady Arculus
Max Reinhardt
Anne Scott-James
Dame Josephine Barnes
Jean Metcalfe
Christopher Fry
Beryl Reid
Odette Hallowes
Dame Barbara Cartland
Elizabeth Jane Howard
Monica Dickens
Keith Waterhouse
Ray Galton
Sir Cyril Smith
Barbara Laming
Lady Longford
Derek Jameson
Marjorie Proops
Spike Milligan
Deirdre, Lady Mountevans
Natasha Kroll
Dulcie Gray
Cleo Laine
Molly Weir
Christina Foyle
Ellen Pollock
John Mortimer
Sir Hugh & Lady Casson
Frances Perry
Sir Edward Heath
Peter O'Sullevan
Richard Johnson
Virginia Graham
Wyn Knowles
Bryan Forbes
Dame Cicely Saunders
Sandy Wilson
Maude Storey
Lady Ricketts
Dorothy Hollingsworth
Sir James Savile
Hubert Gregg
Greville Janner
Dame Jennifer Jenkins
Dame Joan Sutherland
Justin de Blank
Hammond Innes

Wendy Toye
Sir Larry Lamb
Sir Yehudi Menuhin
Bernard Cribbins
Mary Malcolm
Dame Beryl Grey
Sir John Harvey-Jones
Jacquetta Hawkes
Eily Blayney
Katie Boyle
Mary Whitehouse
The Countess Mountbatten
David Langdon
Mrs C P Fairbairn
Dame Margot Smith
Dr Elizabeth Shore
Lord Rix
Max Bygraves
Lady Georgina Coleridge
Daisy Hyams
The Baroness Serota
Fanny Waterman
Ronnie Corbett
David Kossoff
Lady Kennard
Dinah Sheridan
Lady Healey
Ernie Wise
June Whitfield
David Jacobs
Magnus Magnusson
Ann Jellicoe
The Baroness Castle
Pat Koechlin-Smythe
Len Deighton
Chapman Pincher
Stirling Moss
John Schlesinger
Brian Inglis
Lady Redgrave
Sir Harry Llewellyn
Evelyn Anthony
Frank Muir
Sir Clement Freud
Sir Freddie Laker
The Baroness Thatcher
Brian Johnston
Mrs Oliver Lebus
Lady Greenhill
Mary Stott
Sir Harry Secombe

FOREWORD

I am delighted to have been invited to contribute a few words of introduction to this enjoyable cookery book for people over 60. It is so enterprising of the Friends of Elderly Accommodation Counsel to have invited so many elegant, famous and witty men and women, over retirement age, to donate their favourite recipes and tell us why they have selected them.

Cooking should be a pleasure at any time but perhaps even more so when you get older because you can please yourself much more, choosing YOUR favourite foods. Many of the recipes in this book, as their authors tell us, are tried and tested over the years but the contributors have gone out of their way to give us recipes that are quick but tasty, simple but flavourful.

I wish the readers of this book success with these dishes – and a long and happy retirement where good food becomes a pleasureable part of each and every day.

Albert Roux

SOUPS AND STARTERS

NO COOK CHILLED TOMATO SOUP

Dinah
Sheridan

Wonderfully tasty – and no hard work! Just a whoosh in the liquidiser.

Serves 2

1 lb (450 g) tomatoes
1-1½ tbsp chopped onion
½ tsp fresh tarragon (or ¼ tsp if dried)
1 tsp tomato paste
1 tsp sugar
½ tsp salt and pepper
½ x 5 oz (125 g) carton soured cream or plain yoghurt
Chopped chives or parsley

Wash and quarter tomatoes and whisk with the onion, tarragon and tomato paste in a blender until smooth. Stir in the sugar, salt and pepper to taste.

To serve: Put a dollop of cream or yoghurt on top of each bowl and swirl gently. Scatter with chopped chives or parsley.

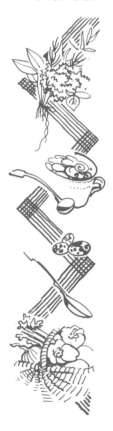

AUNTIE ANNA'S SOUP

This is our favourite family soup. It's delicious, nutritious and very easy to make (if you're a magician!). All you need are lentils and vegetables, plus your choice of stock cubes. We prefer vegetables because we have one or two vegetarians in the family.

Magnus
Magnusson

For a good pot that could keep two folk going all week, you need

8 oz (225 g) lentils

1 potato

2 carrots

1 leek

3 stock cubes

No need to soak the lentils for hours and then boil the life out of them in the old-fashioned way. Put them in a pan with a knob of margarine and a touch of mixed herbs, fry very lightly, then add just enough boiling water to sweat the lentils on a low heat, adding a little water if they look like sticking, until the lentils are soft and pulpy. Sweat the chopped vegetables in the same way in another pan, add them to the lentils with the stock cubes, and top up with water to the required consistency. Simmer for a further twenty minutes.

That's the way Our Anna – Auntie Anna, my sister-in-law – makes soup. The children, now grown up, always demand it when they come home. So do I!

CHILLED SUMMER TOMATO SOUP

The Baroness Castle

One of my favourite summer soup recipes, which is delicious and very easy to prepare – ideal for busy people.

Serves 4

2 tins Campbells tomato soup, concentrated
1 tin tomato juice
1 plain yoghurt
1 chopped onion
1 chopped clove garlic
1 tsp chopped parsley
1 chopped cucumber

Mix all the ingredients in a blender. Leave in a refrigerator to chill.

TOMATO AND ORANGE SOUP

June Whitfield

This is so simple to make and it tastes delicious.

Serves 2

Juice of 2 oranges
Juice of 1 lemon
1¾ pint (1 litre) of tomato juice
1 dstsp Worcester sauce

Boil first 3 ingredients for 5 minutes. Strain and add Worcester sauce. Stir occasionally to prevent burning. Add a pinch of basil if desired.

GREEN PEA SOUP

The mint in the recipe gives the soup a flavour of summer which, even in midwinter, can be so beguiling as to make even the coldest day that bit warmer, but mind you don't burn your tongue in your haste to get at it!

David
Jacobs

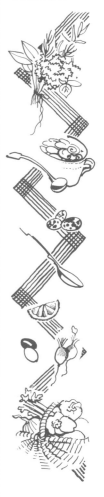

Serves 4

1 bunch spring onions, chopped
1 lb (450 g) packet frozen peas
1 lettuce heart
2 slices of ham, diced
2 tbsp sugar
2 pints (1¼ litre) of stock, made with stock cube
Handful of fresh mint
Butter
Fried croutons
Fresh cream

Soften the onions in butter, add peas, lettuce, ham and sugar. Simmer for 10 minutes. Stir occasionally to avoid burning. Add the stock and mint (keeping some for garnish). Simmer for another 10 minutes. Season and mix in blender to required thickness.

If a thinner soup is required, add more stock.

Serve with a little cream on top with chopped mint and fried croutons.

Cook's Tip: This soup freezes well and is good hot or cold.

MUM'S MINESTRONE

Lady Healey

The best tip I know: get rid of all those old saucepans and frying pans with lids that no longer fit and bent bottoms. Treat yourself to a set of new ones, suitable for your kind of cooker. Choose a set with a steamer included and make sure that the handles are heat resistant and that they do not weigh a ton. Get the best you can afford. Go on – you know you have had the old ones all your life. You have years of happy cooking ahead. Enjoy them.

Serves 2 to 4

2 sticks celery
1 carrot
1 large onion
1 oz (25 g) margarine
1 tin tomatoes
1 cube chicken stock
1 cube beef stock
½ pint (300 ml) water
1 small tin baked beans in tomato sauce
1 bay leaf
1 dstsp fresh basil
1 garlic clove (optional)
2 heaped tbsp chopped parsley

Melt the margarine in a saucepan. Chop the vegetables and gently heat them over a low flame. Add the tinned tomatoes, the beef and chicken stock cubes and the water and slowly cook until the vegetables are done. Add the baked beans, bay leaf, basil, garlic and parsley and slowly simmer.

Serve with grated cheese and crusty bread.

Cook's Tip: Double the quantities and it will feed hungry grandchildren. The basil is essential, fresh if possible. I grow it in pots on the kitchen window sill.

ELIZA ACTON'S APPLE SOUP

'Apples, cherries, hope and women' wrote Dickens 'are the secrets of happiness' – Eliza Acton is thus twice qualified.

Sir Hugh Casson

Serves 6

2 pints (1¼ litres) of beef stock
1 lb (450 g) cooking apples
½ level tsp ground ginger
Salt and black pepper
4 rounded tbsp long grain rice

Wash the apples and chop them roughly without removing peel or core. Bring stock to boil in a large pan, add apples and cover pan with lid. Simmer soup over low heat until apples are tender.

Pour the pulp through a sieve, rubbing through as much as possible of the fruit pulp. Stir in the ginger and season with salt and pepper and reheat.

While the soup is cooking, it should take about 30 minutes, boil the rice in plenty of salted water. Drain thoroughly through a sieve and keep the rice warm. Spoon the soup into bowls and serve the rice separately.

HOT OR COLD GREEN SOUP

Lady
Kennard

Very green. Very healthy. Also delicious and quick to cook.

Serves 2 to 4

| 2 shallots |
| 4 oz (100 g) spinach |
| 2 oz (50 g) sorrel |
| 1 pint (600 ml) stock or 1 chicken cube |
| Cream to taste |

Sweat the shallots in oil. Add the spinach, sorrel and a little stock. Cook gently for 5-10 minutes. Sieve or put in electric mixer. Add rest of stock. Serve hot or cold with cream added to taste.

VEGETABLE SOUP

This is an inexpensive and nourishing soup. The quantity makes enough for two people, so put half in the fridge for another day or invite a friend to lunch.

Serves 2

1 onion, chopped
2 carrots, sliced fairly thinly
A large knob of butter
1 beef stock cube dissolved in ¾ pint (450 ml) of hot water
4 fl oz (125 ml) milk
Pepper and salt

Melt butter in a saucepan. Add vegetables and stir over medium heat for 2 to 3 minutes until they are covered with butter. Cover with half the stock and simmer for about 15 minutes or until vegetables are soft. Liquidise; if you don't have a liquidiser the soup may be sieved. Return to saucepan, stir in the tomato puree and add the rest of the stock and the milk. Season to your own taste and reheat.

Serve with rolls or some hot brown toast.

Cook's Tip: If you have some home made beef stock so much the better, but a Knorr stock cube is very good.

Lady
Elizabeth
Longford

With Barbara
Laming

Pat
Koechlin-
Smythe

GAZPACHO

An easy and excellent recipe that can be kept in the fridge and used with any meal especially in hot weather. This is our standby for summer lunch.

Serves 2 to 4

1 lb (450 g) tomatoes

1 cucumber

1 small onion, according to taste

1 green pepper, according to taste

Some breadcrumbs (I don't use them)

Salt, pepper and paprika

2 tbsp light cooking oil

4 tbsp wine vinegar

Squeeze of lemon

Put all the ingredients in the liquidiser to blend either fine or rougher. Taste and add any ingredients that you want, i.e. more oil or vinegar. Put in ice cubes and leave to cool in fridge.

Serve soup cold with separate bowls of bread cubes (can be fried), tomato, cucumber and onion roughly chopped, so people can add these to their soup as required. Some people like to add water to the soup – we don't.

ONION SOUP

If you know your onions the soup will help to preserve you, which is important over sixty.

Ernie
Wise

Serves 2

1 lb (450 g) onions
Oxo cube
Slice of toast
Grated cheese

Chop onions small. Fry in butter or oil until clear, not brown. Or place in microwave for 2 minutes. Make 1 pint (600 ml) of stock with oxo in a large pan. Add onions, bring to boil and simmer for 1 hour.

Place in soup bowl, float toast covered in cheese on top and put under grill until cheese melts.

QUICK PEA SOUP

This is the easiest recipe I can find!

Greville
Janner

Serves 2 to 3

1 packet frozen peas
1 small onion
1½ pints (900 ml) vegetable or chicken stock (can use cubes)
Salt and pepper

Put all the ingredients in a pan and boil for 5 minutes. Liquidise.

SAVICHE

Chapman
Pincher

Serves 2

Any kind of white fish

1 lemon or lime

Green and red peppers

Chopped spring onions

Place fish in a china or glass bowl. Marinate with lemon or lime. Combine with finely chopped green and red peppers.

Completely cover the bowl to exclude air and place in fridge for 12-24 hours. The fish should then be completely opaque.

Serve decorated with finely chopped spring onions and red peppers.

Cook's Tip: Limes are stronger than lemons.

STUFFED SAVOURY AVOCADO PEARS

Lady
Redgrave

Good food is the staff of life.

Serves 8

2 ripe avocados

4 tbsp French dressing

8 oz (225 g) cottage cheese

4 oz (100 g) chopped spring onions

4 oz (100 g) peeled prawns

Grated rind of ½ lemon

Cut avocados in half, remove stones and brush all over with French dressing. Place on serving dish.

Mix remaining ingredients and season to taste. Spoon in avocados and serve.

TUNA OR SALMON MOUSSE

Not only is this delicious, particularly in summer, but also it is so very simple to make, with virtually no cooking and certainly no specialized knowledge or skills required that I can even make it myself – if pushed!

Stirling Moss

Serves 2 to 4

1 x 8 oz (225 g) packet cream cheese
1 can condensed tomato soup
1 diced green pepper
2 sticks diced celery
1 small grated onion
8 fl oz (250 ml) mayonnaise .
1 large can tuna or salmon
2 tbsp gelatine
4 fl oz (125 ml) cold water

Melt the cream cheese into the tomato soup. When cool, add green pepper, diced celery, onion, mayonnaise and flaked fish.

Dissolve gelatine in cold water. Add to ingredients and pour into mould. Chill until set.

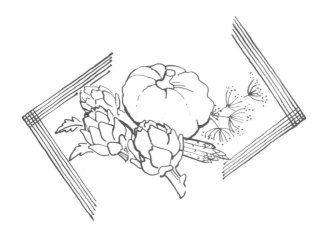

ANCHOVY SHIRRED EGGS

Evelyn
Anthony

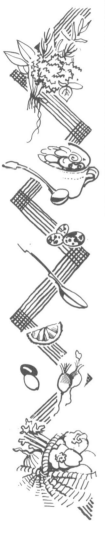

If you make a dish for one if you're alone or better still for two, this is simple, nourishing and a bit wicked – eggs with cream, butter and anchovies. Why not be wicked over 60?

Serves 2

4 free range eggs

2 oz (50 g) butter

1 tbsp single cream

1 dstsp chopped tinned anchovies

Black pepper

Lightly beat the eggs with a whisk, pepper to taste. Do not salt.

Melt butter over heat, add eggs, transfer to low heat and scramble with fork. Before fully cooked, take off heat and add cream. Add anchovies. Serve with buttered toast.

Cook's Tip: Do not overcook. Cream stops the eggs cooking.

LIVER PATE

This is a delicious and well flavoured dish, easy to prepare and suitable either for a main course or a starter.

Dame
Jennifer
Jenkins

Serves 8

8 oz (225 g) minced calves liver
8 oz (225 g) pork sausage meat
8 rashers streaky bacon
2 tsp mixed thyme and parsley
1 small grated onion
1 crushed clove (optional)
1 egg, beaten
4 fl oz (125 ml) stock made from cube
4 bay leaves
Salt and pepper

Line bottom of oven proof dish with bacon. Mix liver and sausagemeat and seasoning. Add beaten egg, then stock. Arrange bay leaves on top. Cover closely. Place in baking tin half full of water.

Cook for 1¼ hours in a moderate oven 375°C (190°F) Gas Mark 5.

WELSH FOIE-GRAS

Sir Harry
Llewellyn

Serves 2 to 4

Fried lambs liver

Marrow extracted from large bones supplied by butcher and melted

Cream to taste

Black olives, chopped with stones removed

Blend all together in equal proportions. Cool before serving.

MACKEREL PATE

Brian
Inglis

It is inexpensive, easy and quick to make and will keep your guests happy while you do the main course.

Serves 2

1 pot soured cream

1 smoked mackerel fillet

1 tsp horseradish sauce (optional)

Mash all the ingredients together with a fork. Do not blend.

TUNA FISH PATE

This recipe is easy and quick to make, delicious – and I've yet to meet anyone who doesn't like tuna fish!

John
Schlesinger

Serves 2 to 4

1 x 7 oz (200 g) tuna fish, drained
1 small tin shrimps or fresh if preferred
1 small tin pimentoes
Lemon juice to taste
Capers to taste
2-3 oz (50-75 g) butter

Place all ingredients in food processor and blend. Add fresh pepper and adjust seasoning to taste. Cayenne pepper is a good addition.

Cook's Tip: If diet is to be considered, yoghurt will work almost as well as butter.

SPINACH AND MUSHROOM ROLL

Dame Barbara Cartland and her chef Nigel Gordon

This is an excellent starter and can be made quickly if people arrive unexpectedly for lunch.

Serves 4

1 lb (450 g) spinach
4 eggs, separated
6 oz (150 g) mushrooms
1 oz (25 g) butter
½ oz (12 g) flour
¼ pint (150 ml) milk
¼ pint (150 ml) cream
Grated nutmeg
Grated parmesan cheese
Salt and pepper

Cook spinach and drain well. Stir in ½ oz of the butter, the egg yolks, salt and pepper.

Whip the whites until firm and fold into the mixture. Spread in a swiss roll tin lined with buttered paper, dust well with parmesan cheese and bake in a hot oven 400°F (200°C) Gas Mark 6 for 15 minutes.

Slice the mushrooms and saute in the rest of the butter, add flour, seasoning, nutmeg, milk and cream and heat slowly without boiling.

Turn out the spinach roll, spread the mushroom mixture over and roll up. Dust with more parmesan cheese and serve with a mushroom sauce.

Handy Hint: Spinach is high in vitamins A and C, both essential to male virility. It is also rich in minerals, particularly iron, calcium and copper. Spinach is on the Chese list of Aphrodisiacs.

WURSTSALAT

Serves 2

8 oz (225 g) Cervelas sausage
4 oz (100 g) tasty cheese
1 hard boiled egg
1 tomato
½ small chopped onion (optional)

Salad dressing

2 tbsp oil
1 tbsp vinegar
½ tsp mild mustard
½ tsp Knorr Aromat
½ tsp Maggi aromatic savoury concentrate sauce
Small quantity of chopped chives or parsley

Cut sausage into half moon shapes and cut cheese, egg and tomato roughly into small dices. Place in a bowl.

To make the dressing, mix all the ingredients together well, add some ground pepper, pour over the salad and toss.

If you have difficulty in obtaining the Knorr Aromat or Maggi sauce, add mild mustard, chives and salt to a vinaigrette sauce.

Serving Suggestion: It is recommended that this salad be eaten with a glass of lager or beer.

Dame Joan Sutherland

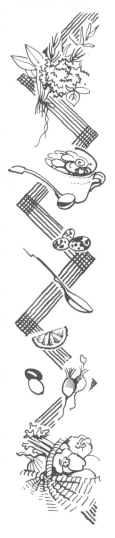

25

Snacks and Suppers

SAUSAGE AND CABBAGE PIE

Justin
de Blank

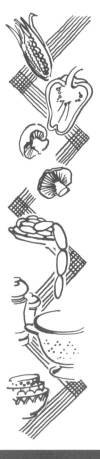

Don't be afraid to make too much of this dish as it reheats perfectly well!

Serves 2

4 large pork sausages, the quality of the sausages is very important
1 small cabbage
Flour
Water
Milk
Grated cheese
Worcestershire sauce (optional)

Bake the sausages in the oven until lightly browned. Cut cabbage in four and half cook in salted water. Remove sausages from baking tin and keep warm. With the fat from the sausages add enough flour to make a crumbly paste. Add half cabbage water and half milk to the paste stirring continuously to form a thick roux. Grate in some cheese. Take a pie dish and mix the sausages with the roux and cabbage until they are well combined, adding Worcestershire sauce if you choose. Grate some more cheese on top and bake in the oven for 20 minutes. Serve steaming hot.

TAGLIATELLE PIE

This has most of the nourishment you need in one meal without adding unwanted calories.

Audrey Slaughter

Serves 2

4 oz (100 g) tagliatelle pasta
1 lb (450 g) leaf spinach
1 egg, beaten
Tomato slices
Grated cheddar cheese

Place pasta in boiling water and cook until tender. Strain and line a small greased pie dish, like a basket. Cook spinach and squeeze to remove water and mix with well beaten egg. Put the mixture into the tagliatelle basket, top with slices of tomato and grated cheese. Dot with butter and bake in oven for 10-15 minutes until cheese has browned and pie is spongy to the touch.

CUCUMBER BAKE

I find that this is extremely popular, being something different.

The Baroness Sharples

Serves 2

1 cucumber
2 oz (50 g) cheddar cheese
¼ pint (150 ml) double cream
Small tin of tomatoes
Salt and pepper

Peel the cucumber and cut into thick slices, put in boiling salted water and cook until tender. Drain well, possibly overnight. Grate the cheese and mix with cream and tomatoes. Cover the cucumber with the sauce, sprinkle some cheese on top and bake in a hot oven, 350°F (180°C) Gas Mark 4 for 20 minutes.

CABBAGE AND BACON COTTAGE PIE

Ray
Galton

This was the recipe I loved my Granny to make during the war. I still look forward to my wife making it, especially as the ingredients don't cost an arm and a leg.

1 lb (450 g) potatoes
2 lb (1 kg) cabbage or brussels sprouts
4 oz (100 g) streaky bacon or ham or leftover pork
Fat for frying
1 oz (25 g) butter
Small quantity of milk, salt and pepper

Preheat oven to 325°F (160°C) Gas Mark 3. Cook potatoes and cabbage separately. Cut bacon into small pieces and fry in fat. Mix bacon and cabbage and put into pie dish. Mash potatoes with milk, butter, salt and pepper. Cover bacon and cabbage with mashed potatoes and put into preheated oven for 20 minutes.

CHEESE AND BACON SAVOURY

Lady
Grade

This was one of my mother's favourite recipes and it brings back so many happy memories of my childhood when my mother used to make it for us on cold winter evenings.

Serves 2

4 slices of lean bacon
½ medium sized onion, finely chopped
2½ oz (60 g) cheddar cheese, grated
1 level tsp plain flour
4 fl oz (125 ml) semi-skimmed milk
3 tbsp oil
Pepper

Fry bacon in oil, then remove from pan. Fry onion until transparent, do not let it go brown. Stir in flour, gradually adding milk. When mixture has thickened, add cheese until melted. Put the slices of bacon back into the mixture and add pepper. The dish is now ready to be served on buttered toast.

STIR FRY

I soon realised after my wife died that a good deal of culinary effort was to fall on my shoulders! This calamity appalled me. I became riddled with self pity, until a samaritan presented me with a wok, which changed my life. I was always busy in my studio and to have to slave in the kitchen on a mid-day meal was simply not on. My precious wok solved this problem. Whatever I seemed to find and sling into the sizzling bowl ended up a quickly produced and delightful repast. I use it often.

Terence Cuneo

Serves 2

1 tbsp oil
2 pkts stir fry mix
Any left over vegetables, bacon, egg, etc

Take a wok, or large frying pan, add oil and stir fry mixture and add anything such as odd pieces of meat, vegetables, sweetcorn, orange or an apple. Stir it at a fairly high heat for about 7 or 8 minutes and serve immediately.

Cook's Tip: This is a good way to use up leftovers.

COURGETTE SALAD

For recipes I cannot do better than refer you to my wife's charming little book, HOME IS MY GARDEN, written just before she died and published under her married name, Dorothy Hammond Innes. Here is just one of many quotes:

Hammond Innes

Courgettes make a lovely and quite substantial salad. They are good raw, but I prefer them put in boiling water for not more than five minutes, so they don't lose their firmness. When cold I slice them into rounds, dress them with a lot of marjoram, olive oil and lemon, black pepper and coarse salt.

ONION OMELETTE

Max
Reinhardt

I hope people will enjoy my onion omelette as much as I do.

Serves 1

3 medium onions
1 tbsp oil
2 medium eggs
Salt and pepper
1 tbsp water
1 oz (25 g) butter

Peel and roughly chop onions. Place in frying pan with oil, preferably using a pan with a lid. Cook onions over medium heat until soft and brown. Onions should be stirred occasionally. While onions are cooking, place eggs, seasoning and water together in a small bowl. Mix until frothy.

When onions are cooked, put aside. Using same hot pan but without lid, add butter. Pour in eggs. When edges are brown move the pan so that the liquid centre reaches the edge and is cooked.

While the eggs are still softish, slip the omelette onto a heated plate. Place onions in the centre and fold omelette over. Eat immediately.

OEUFS EN COCOTTES WITH SPINACH AND HAM

This recipe is quick to make but it is not 'fast food'. Eggs and spinach are light and healthy and the ham adds a bit of substance.

Anne
Scott-James

Serves 2 as a main dish or 4

4 eggs
Savoury mixture: spinach puree and chopped ham *or* chopped cooked mushrooms *or* creamed sweetcorn
Knob of butter
Salt and pepper
Cream (optional)

Butter four fireproof cocottes or ramekins, put a little savoury mixture in each, then add an egg on top being careful not to break the yolk. I usually break each egg into a cup first then slide it into the dish. Stand the dishes in a pan with a little hot water in it, not more than an inch, cover them with greaseproof paper and bake in a moderate oven for about five minutes. The whites should be just set but the yolks must not set hard. If you have any cream float a little on the top of each dish, add a tiny bit of salt and pepper and serve with teaspoons.

31

HAM AND CELERY ROLLS

Lady
Arculus

6 slices of ham
1 tin celery hearts
1 small tin peeled tomatoes
4 oz (100 g) grated cheddar cheese
Salt and pepper

Roll each slice of ham around one third of a heart of celery and place side by side in a dish. Pour over tomatoes, chopped if required. Add salt and pepper, cover with grated cheese and put in moderate oven, 375°F (190°C) Gas Mark 5, until cheese is browned.

Serve with country bread and green salad.

Variation: Asparagus spears can be used as an alternative to celery hearts.

RICE PILAU

Dame
Josephine
Barnes

My recipe is for those in a hurry and with limited facilities. It can be cooked on a single gas or electric ring. If I come in late or am in a hurry it can be prepared within about 15 minutes.

Serves 1

1 dstsp oil
2-3 oz (50-75 g) rice
4-6 fl oz (125-180 ml) boiling water
½ tsp salt
Cooked ham or any leftovers
4 oz (100 g) frozen peas or beans

Fry rice with salt in oil. Add boiling water and bring mixture to boil. Add ham or leftovers and frozen vegetables. Stir and cover tightly for 10 minutes on low heat or until rice is cooked.

Opposite:
Lady Kennard's Hot
or Cold Green Soup

CHICORY AND HAM IN CHEESE SAUCE

This is a one-dish recipe and anything left over reheats beautifully. No other vegetables needed and we love chicory.

Jean Metcalfe

Serves 2

2 medium heads chicory

2 slices ham

Cheese sauce

1 oz (25 g) butter

1 oz (25 g) plain flour

¾ pint (450 ml) milk or mixture of milk and chicory stock

6 oz (150 g) grated cheese

Extra grated cheese for topping

Cover cleaned chicory heads in water or light stock spiked with lemon juice and cook until tender but still firm. Drain retaining liquor. Make up cheese sauce by melting butter in a pan, stir in flour and then slowly add milk or stock and milk mixture. When sauce is smooth stir in cheese.

Wrap each head of chicory in a slice of ham. Lay them in a buttered ovenproof dish. Cover with sauce. Top with grated cheese. Bake in the oven at 350°F (180°C) Gas Mark 4 for about 30 minutes or until bubbling and browned on top.

Serve with chunks of crusty bread to mop up the sauce!

Opposite:
Lady Redgrave's Stuffed Savoury Avocado Pears

Elizabeth
Jane
Howard

EGG IN A BUN

This recipe is nourishing, simple to make but unusual and festive enough to serve to a friend for supper with perhaps some spinach. This dish would also be popular with grandchildren who like the idea of an egg in a bun.

Serves 1

1 round soft bread roll
¼ oz (7 g) butter
¼ oz (7 g) grated cheese
1 egg, separated
Salt and pepper

Heat the oven to 350°F (180°C) Gas Mark 4. Cut the top off the bun, scoop out the soft part from the bottom, butter the inside and put it in the oven for about 5 minutes to make it crisp. Then put half the grated cheese inside the bun and put egg yolk on top.

Turn up oven to 400°F (200°C) Gas Mark 6. Whisk the white stiffly, add the rest of the cheese to it and put mixture on top of bun. Bake in the oven until the white is set.

Serving Suggestion: You may want to eat two eggs, in which case you double the quantities.

ACTOR'S TEA

Teach your children to teach their children's children that everything stops for tea.

David
Kossoff

Serves 1

1 tin herring in tomato sauce
1 spanish onion
Salt and pepper
Vinegar or lemon juice

Mash up the contents of the tin. Slice and cut the onion and mix in. Add vinegar or lemon juice, salt and pepper to taste. Serve with or on buttered toast.
   No cooking to do!

SAUSAGES IN CIDER

Sausages are a good thing and cider is a good thing and sausages in cider has the virtues of each and the agreeability of both.

Christopher
Fry

Serves 4

1 lb (450 g) sausages
2 cooking apples
1 lb (450 g) onions
1 tbsp mustard
½-1 pint (300-600 ml) dry cider

Brown the sausages either by lightly frying or grilling. Fry the onions in a little oil, add the mustard. Add the chopped up apples and mix up altogether with the sausages. Then pour over the cider and cook gently over a low flame.

STUFFED AUBERGINE

Mary
Malcolm

I chose this recipe because aubergine is not expensive and you can omit the ham without spoiling the finished dish.

Serves 2

1 aubergine

1 red pepper

1 green pepper

1 yellow pepper

1 clove garlic

Sprinkle of parsley

Olive oil

Salt and pepper

Boil the aubergine until you can stick a fork in easily. Drain and cool. While aubergine is cooking, deseed and finely chop peppers. When aubergine is cooked, cut in half and scoop out all the flesh. Mash it up and add the chopped peppers, chopped garlic and parsley. Season well with salt and pepper and stir in olive oil to taste.

This is delicious wrapped in ham, put in pastry tartlets or wrapped in pancakes. Or it makes a pleasant side dish to serve with a mixed salad.

ROTMOS –
Swedish Mashed Turnips

Dame
Beryl
Grey

This recipe is easy to make, costs little yet is both delicious, nutritious and unusual. It can accompany meat, fish or vegetarian mixtures or simply be enjoyed on its own.

Serves 2

8 oz (225 g) potatoes

12 oz (300 g) turnips

¼ pint (150 ml) stock or water

4 tbsp cream (optional)

1 tbsp butter

½ tsp sugar

Salt and pepper

Wash, peel and cube turnips and potatoes. Cook turnips in stock or slightly salted water for 30 minutes, add potatoes and cook until soft, approximately a further 30 minutes.

Drain, mash and add cream. Season, then beat until smooth and finally stir in cold butter.

SINGLE MAN'S LUNCH

Because of the serious national water shortage this meal can be consumed from the can or pan and does not need washing up afterwards.

Serves 1

1 can beans
1 can soup

Pour into pan. Heat and eat straight from pan. No washing up.

Being a single man this is important.

Sir James
Savile

WELCH RAREBIT

Serves 2

9 oz (225 g) Red Leicester cheese
Dry mustard
Beer or milk
Bread to toast
Worcester sauce

Odette
Hallowes

Cut cheese into squares and place in non stick saucepan. Add teaspoon of mustard and two soup spoonfuls of beer or milk. Stir slowly. When melted, pour over toast and grill until slightly brown. Then remove from grill and add a few drops of Worcester sauce over cheese.

SPAGHETTI DOLCE

Spike
Milligan

Serves 2

Spaghetti, cooked al dente, no salt

5 oz (125 g) double cream

2 tbsp brandy

Caster sugar to taste

Cook spaghetti for about 8 minutes. Whilst this is cooking mix together cream, brandy and castor sugar. When spaghetti is ready, pour over the cream mixture. Serve straight away.

SAUSAGES IN OXTAIL

Beryl
Reid

Serves 4

1 lb (450 g) thick sausages

1 lb (450 g) onions

Little oil for frying

1 tin oxtail soup

Grill or bake sausages or use a trivet so that fat runs away. In a large saucepan, fry the onions for about 20 minutes until tender.

When sausages are cooked, cut them into 1 inch pieces and add them to the cooked onions and the soup and reheat.

Serve on mashed potatoes.

CORNED BEEF PIE

It's simple and easy to get on with. A bit like me really – no complications!

Serves 2

1 large tin Fray Bentos corned beef
1 large onion
2 lb (1 kg) potatoes
1 pint (600 ml) Oxo beef stock
8 oz (225 g) short crust pastry

Cut corned beef into cubes. Chop onion and place in pan with beef stock. Cook until onions are soft. Boil potatoes until cooked.

Drain beef stock from corned beef and onions and save. Drain liquid from potatoes and mash. Mix all the ingredients.

Line tin plate with half the short crust pastry and pile on beef mixture. Cover pie with remaining pastry. Bake in oven at 350°F (180°C) Gas Mark 5 for 35 minutes or until pastry is golden brown. Finally make a gravy with leftover stock from beef and onion.

Sir Cyril Smith

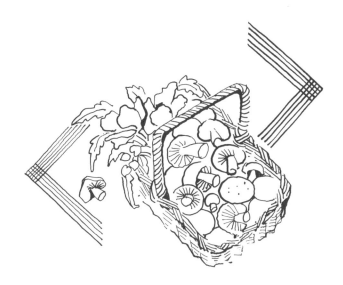

EASY LASAGNE

Lady
Longford
With
Barbara
Laming

This dish is easy to make because it is not necessary to pre-cook the lasagne, nor is there a fussy sauce to make. Also it is a complete meal in itself.

Serves 4

1 lb (450 g) good quality mince or ground beef

1 onion, chopped

4-5 lasagne leaves

1 level dstsp curry powder

1 tin tomatoes

3-4 oz (75-100 g) cheese

1 tbsp unsweetened dessicated coconut

Brush a thick based saucepan with oil. Put in the meat and sprinkle with curry powder. Stir on a medium heat until the meat is brown. Mix in the onion and add tomatoes. Put a layer of the meat in the oven proof dish and then a layer of lasagne – I prefer to break up the lasagne a little – and continue with layers, finishing with a meat layer. Cover and put in a low oven for about an hour until meat is cooked.

While the meat is cooking, prepare topping. Grate the cheese and mix with coconut. Sprinkle over the top of the dish and return to the oven uncovered. Serve when the top is nice and brown.

JON'S JOY

Serves 2

1 tin mushroom soup

2 handfuls shell pasta

1 x 7 oz (200 g) tin tuna fish

2 tbsp breadcrumbs

1 tbsp grated cheese

Cook the pasta in boiling salted water until soft. Heat the soup. Have a deep dish ready warmed and put in cooked pasta, soup and tuna, stir them all together. Top with breadcrumbs and cheese. Heat in a medium oven 350°F (180°C) Gas Mark 4, until top is beginning to brown. Serve with a green salad.

Ann
Jellicoe

PICK-ME-UP

Juice of 1 orange

1 raw egg

4 fl oz (125 ml) skimmed milk

Mix together in a blender until frothy. Add a little wheatgerm, sprinkled on top.

Perfect for breakfast or even lunch when recovering from an illness with little appetite.

Audrey
Slaughter

THE PERFECT LUNCH FOR ELDERLY AUTHORS

Frank
Muir

Take one slice of bread from a new loaf not more than three hours old (preferably Hovis but *not* wholemeal which has bits of toffee in it).

Place in electric toaster and activate switch.

Turn the slice of bread every 20 seconds. First upside down, then back to front, then switch places with the slices and repeat. Wear gloves if fingers begin to blister.

When the toast is golden brown, the colour of a good potato crisp, remove and butter moderately. Use a country butter, slightly salted, at blood heat, and butter smoothly right up to the edges of the crusts.

Take a block of fresh, mild, cheddar cheese, preferably from the West Country but some East Anglian cheeses are tolerable in an emergency. Carefully slice into pieces exactly three sixteenths of an inch thick. Make a trial slice first and test thickness with calipers. Assemble the slices of cheese on the buttered surface of the toast in such a manner that the surface is exactly covered. In no circumstances must the cheese protrude beyond the perimeters of the toast. Use a sharp knife to trim off any surplus, working widdershins, i.e., in an anti-clockwise direction. Nor should gaps be left so that buttered toast is visible between the interterstices of the pieces of cheese. Tweezers can be helpful in easing small wedges of cheese into the chinks.

Carefully spread on top of the cheese a half tablespoonful of marmalade. Home-made, of course, and rough cut. Try to obtain navel oranges grown on the hill area eight miles north of Cadiz; the zest has a fluted aftertaste which complements the confident, almost jaunty, flavour of the juice.

Eat.

Who says that a man cannot make himself a simple meal?

FISH DISHES

SEAFOOD PASTA

I have delighted in pasta ever since I discovered, when living in Italy for a year that pasta isn't fattening. With seafood it's like slimming in the company of mermaids.

Christopher Fry

Serves 2

2 oz (50 g) butter
2 garlic cloves
1 pack frozen mixed seafood or tin of mussels, cockles, etc
2 or 3 tbsp single cream
Lemon juice
4 oz (100 g) pasta shells
Salt and pepper

Cook pasta shells according to instructions on packet and drain. Approximately 12 minutes. Melt butter over low heat and add garlic, which has been chopped and crushed with salt. Add cooked pasta and thawed seafood, seasoning and good squeeze of lemon. Stir until hot, add cream and stir to heat cream.

Serve garnished with chopped parsley. Should be eaten soon after preparation.

FISH PIE

John
Mortimer

The unwholesome and repellent food at school led me, in my schooldays, to cook omelettes according to Marcel Boulestin's instructions ('Always get the pan so hot that the almond-sized pat of butter jumps about when placed in it') over the study fire.

Since then I have cooked assiduously, and a major irritant for any lady who has ever lived with me has been that she is only grudgingly allowed into the kitchen.

I think that English food, properly understood, is by far the best in the world, and I have chosen the most resolutely dull English dish in my repertoire: in fact, it's delicious.

Fish pie fills everyone up, and allows you to talk to them without a constant dash from the room to have a look at the flaming grill or the collapsing soufflé.

Cooking it has a remarkably soothing effect after a day at the Old Bailey, and many plots occur to you whilst peeling the potatoes.

Cook to the accompaniment of a private bottle of Sancerre and *Any Questions* on the radio.

This programme provides the element of frustrated loathing and rage which is missing in the dish itself.

Serves 4

1 lb (450 g) cod or any white fish – ask fishmonger to skin it
1 oz (25 g) butter
1 oz (25 g) flour
½ pint (300 ml) milk
7 eggs
1 small onion
Fresh parsley
4 oz (100 g) prawns (frozen will do)
1 jar mussels
1 lb (450 g) potatoes
Salt and pepper, grated cheese and breadcrumbs

Grill the fish – this is important as it gives far more flavour than steaming it.

Make a white sauce with the butter, flour and milk.

Hardboil 6 eggs, and add them (sliced with onion and

chopped parsley) to the white sauce.

Add the fish when it's cooked, together with the prawns and mussels, and put the lot into a buttered ovenproof dish.

Now cream the potatoes over a low heat with a lot of butter and seasoning, break 1 egg into it, and stir.

Also add grated cheese to give flavour to the potatoes.

Make a cover for the fish with the potatoes, and sprinkle with breadcrumbs.

Cook in the oven at 350°F (180°C) Gas Mark 4 until golden brown.

Serve with hard white cabbage which you should cook with a lot of butter (add a cup of water only in the last few minutes), and red cabbage cooked in brown sugar, vinegar, and beer.

Open another bottle of Sancerre and turn off *Any Questions*.

TROUT WITH DILL

Serves 2

2 medium trout
Bunch fresh dill
1 small tsp salt
Slice of lemon
Few peppercorns
5 fl oz (150 ml) mayonnaise, mild
1 egg white

Deirdre
Lady
Mountevans

Place trout in shallow ovenproof dish with 2 sprigs of dill inside each fish. Add peppercorns, lemon and salt and a little water. Cover with foil and place in preheated oven at 375°F (190°C) Gas Mark 5 for 25 minutes. Cool fish in liquid. Remove dill and skin from trout.

Arrange on serving dish, garnish with dill, lemon and cucumber slices. Whisk egg white until stiff and fold in mayonnaise. Chop dill finely and add to mayonnaise.

Serve with thin brown bread and salad.

Serving Suggestion: Tiny chopped mushrooms or finely sliced courgettes can also be used in small quantities.

This dish can be prepared beforehand.

RUSSIAN SALAD WITH HERRING AND BEETROOT

Natasha Kroll

With slices of bread and butter this makes a light, spicy and nourishing lunch or supper dish. No cooking required.

Serves 1

1 small boiled beetroot
1 small boiled potato, peeled
1 fillet of pickled or Matjes herring
1 small dill pickle or sweet and sour cucumber
½ small tart apple, cored and peeled
2 oz (50 g) ham, optional
1 hard boiled egg, cut into quarters
3 oz (75 g) soured cream or yoghurt mixed with 1 tsp mustard

Cut the beetroot, potato, herring, dill pickle, apple and ham into ¼ inch dice and mix together in a bowl. Add soured cream and toss together thoroughly but lightly until all ingredients are well moistened.

Heap onto a large plate and place quartered egg on top.

SALMON MAYONNAISE

Ellen Pollock

Serves 4

3 lb (1.5 kg) tail of salmon
16 new potatoes
1 curly lettuce
1 orange
1 apple
½ cucumber
Hellman's mayonnaise

Brush salmon with oil or melted butter. Wrap in foil and place in large frying pan half filled with cold water. Cover and bring to the boil. Allow to boil (not too fiercely) for 10 minutes and leave to cool for about 20 minutes.

Boil new potatoes in their skins until tender, approx 15 minutes.

Slice orange, apple and cucumber and arrange all on a large flat dish and add mayonnaise.

DEIGHTON ON FISH

I travel a great deal to research my books and like to be with my family. Recently we spent six months in Austria where the kitchen had no oven. So we know some of the problems faced by retired people.

Len Deighton

In Portugal we eat a great deal of fish and we all enjoy it very much. I wanted this contribution to be of practical use so I have suggested some simple fish meals that need little or no cooking. Some experienced cooks may feel that what I've proposed is too elementary but I have in mind men who have suddenly been faced with the problems of cooking for themselves. I have found that men especially enjoy smoked fish. The ladies will perhaps be converted to it.

SMOKED FISH: Smoked fish are a high protein food in a digestible form, and they keep reasonably well. Kippers, smoked haddock and buckling are delicious. These are excellent for people living alone. Smoked fish is already cooked, and only needs warming through. Fish oils are good for health so don't avoid oily fish on that account. It is worth the time and trouble to find a good reliable shop from which to buy these fish. In the case of kippers and haddock ask for undyed ones for preference.

BUCKLING: These delicious smoked herrings are eaten cold so it's the easiest meal of all. They vary in plumpness and flavour according to the season. When they are good they are better than smoked salmon. Some people find the bones a drawback but I think picking them out is worth the trouble. Smoked trout can be eaten the same way but I marginally prefer the buckling. Both these are often served with thin brown bread and butter and a piece of lemon to squeeze over the top.

KIPPER: If I am alone and working hard I make a quick and delicious meal by putting a kipper into a jug and then pouring boiling water on to it. After five minutes drain the fish and serve it. (You might prefer to buy filleted kippers.) For a more eleborate meal scrambled egg provides a very good accompaniment to the kippers. Don't forget the wholemeal bread and the butter.

If I have more time, and the facilities, I like to grill the kippers. I never put oil or butter or anything at all on them before cooking them as kippers have oil enough already.

SMOKED HADDOCK: Can be cooked in a jug of boiling water but it is more usual to bake it. Using an oven dish put the haddock in a little water (or water with milk), cover with greaseproof paper or tinfoil and bake it in the oven for 10-15 minutes. A small knob of butter improves the haddock because this is not an oily fish. A softly-boiled egg, boiled for about three minutes, broken over the haddock makes a delicious sauce for it.

Equally delicious are smoked mackerel and smoked sprats. What about smoked salmon you say. I like it very much indeed and I still think Irish smoked salmon is the best I've ever tasted. But in my experience three quarters of the smoked salmon on sale is not worth eating and certainly not worth the fancy prices charged for it. If you can get good smoked salmon and can afford it, eat it and good luck.

Try pickled fish. For instance: roll mops in jars. These are filleted herrings pickled in vinegar, look for a good brand for they can be extremely good and a bargain. In the pickle they will keep for a few days. Nowadays many delicatessen counters sell other sorts of pickled herring. For instance there is herring in sour cream into which I like to mix pieces of raw peeled dessert apple. No matter that it sounds unusual: it is delicious and a popular dish in many countries. Smoked eel is my favourite smoked fish but it is very expensive and hard to find. Lastly don't despise the humble tin of sardines. In my family this is a very popular lunch.

HERRINGS IN OATMEAL

Dulcie Gray

This is very simple to cook and can be eaten for breakfast, a light lunch or supper. For people who aren't enthusiastic cooks or who are very busy, an easy meal is sometimes a good idea. It certainly is for me.

Serves 4

4 small filleted herrings
2 tbsp plain flour
½ tsp dry mustard
¼ tsp salt
¼ tsp black pepper

Opposite: Max Reinhardt's Onion Omelette

1 egg, beaten

2 oz (50 g) fine oatmeal

2 tbsp olive oil

1½ oz (40 g) butter

Juice of 1 lemon

Dust the herring fillets in a mixture of flour, salt, pepper and mustard. Dip fish fillets into beaten egg, then coat evenly with oatmeal. Heat butter and olive oil and fry fillets for 3 minutes each side. Don't overcook. Drain on absorbent paper and serve hot with lemon juice squeezed over them.

Serving Suggestion: This dish is very good with scrambled eggs.

BAKED HADDOCK AU GRATIN

Serves 4

Frances
Perry

1 lb (450 g) filleted haddock, cut into 4 portions

8 oz (225 g) packet frozen spinach

3 oz (75 g) finely grated cheese

½ tsp salt

Pinch of pepper

3 tbsp milk, plus a little extra milk

1 oz (25 g) butter or margarine

1 oz (25 g) plain flour

Place fish portions in a greased baking dish, sprinkle with salt and pepper and 3 tbsp of milk. Cover with foil. Bake in preheated oven at 350°F (180°C) Gas Mark 4 for 12 minutes until just cooked. Cook spinach according to instructions on packet.

Remove fish from dish and put cooked spinach into dish with fish on top. Use liquid from fish and the extra milk, about ½ pint (300 ml) liquid, to make the sauce. Melt butter, add flour and liquid gradually. Bring to the boil stirring well. Add half the cheese. Pour over the fish. Sprinkle with the rest of the cheese and brown under a hot grill or in oven.

Opposite:
Christopher Fry's
Seafood Pasta

49

FISH PIE

Molly
Weir

This is my favourite fish pie, it can be concocted from the smallest piece of left-over Finnan Haddy, a single hard-boiled egg and two or three tablespoons of mashed potato. Quick, easy, economical and delicious and with its white sauce a real touch of the 'cordon bleus' about it! Waste not want not was the lesson of my grannie and of the war years, and this moreish recipe does that very thing most agreeably.

Serves 2

8 oz (225 g) white fish or any left over white or smoked fish
2 oz (50 g) butter
A little flour
1 or 2 hard boiled eggs
Creamy mashed potato made with milk and butter

Make a good white sauce by melting butter in a pan, then remove pan from heat and stir in a spoonful or two of flour to make a roux. Add a little milk and any fish stock in which the fish was cooked. Return pan to heat, stir until the sauce is smooth and thick. Season to taste with salt and pepper. Add shelled, boiled roughly chopped eggs. Fold in the cooked fish, flaked into smaller pieces and transfer to heat proof shallow dish and cover with mashed potato. Heat through in the oven at 375°F (190°C) Gas Mark 5 until potatoes are lightly browned. Cover with grated cheese if you wish and slip dish under grill to finish.

HADDOCK WITH CUCUMBER

This is an apology to the Haddock we both hated, Haddock at School and now it is one of our favourite dishes – we hope it will become yours too.

Sir Hugh
and
Lady Casson

Serves 2

4 frozen haddock steaks or fillets
1 cucumber
6 fl oz (180 ml) orange juice
1½ oz (40 g) margarine or butter
1 tbsp flour
3 tbsp cream
Seasoning to taste
Chopped parsley

Place fish in a shallow ovenproof dish, peel cucumber and cut into ½ inch chunks. Place these around the fish and pour the orange juice over the lot. Cover dish with foil and bake in pre-heated oven for about 25 minutes.

Melt the butter in a pan, stir in flour, remove pan from heat and pour in liquid from the cooked fish. Stir until smooth, add seasoning, bring to the boil and add the cream and parsley. Pour over the fish and cucumber and serve.

CRISPY TANGY FISH

Christina
Foyle

I decided on this dish for a recipe book for the over 60's because it is very light to digest and at the same time delicious. It is very simple to make and inexpensive. I have it once a week.

Serves 2

½ oz (12 g) butter

2 tbsp plain flour

¼ pint (150 ml) milk

1 tbsp salad cream

½ tsp lemon juice

Salt and pepper

8 oz (225 g) white fish fillet

1 oz (25 g) dry breadcrumbs

1 oz (25 g) streaky bacon, rind removed and chopped

1 oz (25 g) cheddar cheese, grated

Melt the butter in a pan, stir in the flour and cook for 1 minute. Gradually blend in the milk and heat stirring until the sauce thickens. Stir in the salad cream, lemon juice and salt and pepper to taste.

Divide fish into two pieces, place in shallow oven-proof dish and pour over sauce. Combine breadcrumbs, bacon and cheese and sprinkle over sauce.

Cook in a pre-heated moderately hot oven 375°F (190°C) Gas Mark 5 for about 20 minutes. Place under a pre-heated grill for 2-3 minutes.

CLEO'S FISH STEW

It's simple, economical and very nutritious and the ingredients can be varied to what is available.

Cleo
Laine

Serves 2

½ pint (300 ml) water
4 tbsp wine vinegar or lemon juice
1 small onion, sliced
1 celery stick, sliced
1 medium carrot, sliced
Any other vegetables to be used up
Fish or vegetable stock cube
Salt and pepper
1 bay leaf, pinch of thyme or other herbs to taste
3-4 sprigs fresh parsley
Few prawns, crab sticks, mussels or any sea food
½-¾ lb (225-300 g) white fish pieces, skinned and boned
Cornflour (optional)

Combine all the ingredients together except fish. Bring to the boil then reduce heat and simmer for at least 30 minutes. Add white fish, stir and cook until fish is tender. Add seafood, cook for a few minutes more, then serve.

Use a small amount of cornflour to thicken if required.

Cook's Tip: Use any leftover fish the fishmonger has. He will bone and skin it. This makes the ingredients relatively inexpensive. You can make double the quantity and freeze half the stew. For a special touch add dry white wine and a little cream.

53

CHICKEN DISHES

CHICKEN BREASTS AU GRATIN

Maude
Storey

If, like me you have never been busier than in retirement or just as desirably enjoying sitting back and letting it all happen – this is the dish for you. Suitable as a meal for one or for serving to many, it's easy to prepare, looks appetising, highly nutritious protein and can be served straight from the oven – minimal washing up!

Serves 1

1 boneless chicken breast
Flour to coat chicken breast
½ oz (12 g) butter
1 oz (25 g) cheese – Emmenthal or processed cheese slice
2 tbsp chicken or vegetable stock
Salt and pepper

Flatten the chicken breast with a rolling pin. Sprinkle breast with salt and pepper and coat very lightly in flour.

Melt butter in frying pan and saute chicken for about 5 minutes each side until golden brown.

Remove from heat and transfer to ovenproof dish. Lay a cheese slice over the chicken, pour over stock and transfer to oven for about 20 minutes at 350°F (180°C) Gas Mark 4.

Increase portions for additional persons.

PIQUANT CHICKEN BREASTS

This dish is enhanced for both palate and conscience by use of free-range chickens which have more flavour and have not been victims of life imprisonment in a battery cage.

Peter
O'Sullevan

Serves 6

6 chicken breasts

Marinade

2 tsp Dijon mustard

1 tsp dried Provence herbs

4 tbsp oil

2 tsp Worcester sauce

Pinch cayenne pepper

Juice of 1 lemon

Make a cut crosswise on each chicken breast and put them in a fireproof shallow dish. Prepare marinade by mixing all the ingredients and pour over chicken breasts. Leave for 6-8 hours or overnight, turning the breasts and brushing them with the marinade from time to time.

Preheat oven to 425°F (220°C) Gas Mark 7 and place chicken dish in middle of hot oven for 35-45 minutes.

By that time the chicken should be crisp and brown outside and succulent inside.

Should be a 'winner' too!

BAKED CHICKEN WITH LEEKS

Wyn
Knowles

I would like to share the wonderful combination of flavours of chicken and leeks which I discovered when needing to make a meal from what I happened to have in my fridge.

Serves 2

2-3 leeks

2 chicken joints

2 oz (50 g) butter

2 tbsp stock or water

Bouquet Garni (if available fresh – 1 bay leaf, sprig parsley and thyme)

Salt and Pepper

Wash leeks thoroughly and chop white part and parts of the more delicate green leaves.

Melt butter in a pan and saute leeks for a few minutes until softened.

Place the remaining butter in a shallow ovenproof dish. Put chicken joints on top of leeks and add stock, bouquet garni, salt and pepper. Baste chicken and place in oven at 400°F (200°C) Gas Mark 6 and cook for 30-35 minutes.

MRS PEABODY'S CHICKEN

Virginia
Graham

This is a wonderful recipe for a very bad cook, such as I am since it's dead easy to follow and always turns out delicious.

Serves 4

4 chicken breasts

1 x 6 oz (150 g) tin mushrooms

1 x 10 oz (275 g) tin mushroom soup

½ soup tin sherry

1 carton sour cream

Grated onion

Arrange chicken in shallow baking dish and cover with mushrooms. Mix soup, sherry and sour cream and pour over. Sprinkle with grated onion. This is so easy even I can do it!

Bake for 1½ hours at 350°F (180°C) Gas Mark 4.

HONEYED CHICKEN

Serves 2

2 chicken breasts

6 dried apricots, chopped (the sort you don't need to soak)

1 tbsp clear honey

4 tbsp oil

2 tbsp lemon juice

Salt and pepper

Mix all the ingredients, except the chicken. Place chicken in dish and pour over the mixture. Leave for a few hours or overnight, in the fridge.

Bake in hot oven at 350°F (180°C) Gas Mark 4 for about 30 minutes or until chicken is tender. Serve with rice.

Bryan
Forbes

CHICKEN ANNA

This recipe uses up leftovers, it is easy to make, looks pretty – and is delicious to eat!

Serves 2

Left over cold chicken

Curry sauce

Mayonnaise

Parsley

Make about ¼ pint (150 ml) of curry sauce with chicken stock or a stock cube. When cool, mix with mayonnaise to form a cream and add chopped parsley.

Arrange sliced chicken on dish, cover with sauce. Serve with salad and boiled new potatoes.

Sandy
Wilson

Dame
Cicely
Saunders

CHICKEN PILAFF

This recipe is one of my husband's favourites. It takes very little time to make and is very easy for the elderly to eat.

Serves 2

1 oz (25 g) butter
Small spanish onion, chopped
1 clove garlic, chopped
1 green pepper, finely chopped
2 oz (50 g) almond flakes
8 oz (225 g) tin pineapple chunks
5-6 oz (125-150 g) long grain rice
8 oz (225 g) diced cooked chicken
½ pint (300 ml) chicken stock, Knorr instant will do
1 tbsp fresh parsley
Salt and parsley

Melt the butter slowly in a large saucepan which has a well fitting lid. Gently saute the onion, garlic and green pepper to soften, then add the almonds and let them cook for a minute or two.

Stir in the rice and allow it to absorb all the butter and juices and then add the chicken pieces. Pour on the stock, add seasoning, give a good stir and put the lid on.

Simmer gently on a low heat for about 20 minutes or until all the liquid is absorbed.

Add the pineapple and let that heat through which takes about 10 minutes.

Serve with freshly chopped parsley sprinkled over and a fresh salad.

CHICKEN IN LEMON AND REDCURRANT JELLY SAUCE

I chose this recipe because I'm not a good cook, it's simple, I've never known it go wrong and you can prepare it and cook it later.

Wendy Toye

Serves 4

4 chicken portions
Grated rind and juice of 1 lemon
2 tbsp cooking oil
1 clove garlic, optional
3 tbsp redcurrant jelly
1 tbsp mixed dried herbs
1 tbsp fresh parsley, chopped
Salt and pepper

Place chicken joints in suitable ovenproof dish. Place all the other ingredients in a bowl and mix together. Spoon sauce over the chicken and leave to marinate for 1 hour or longer, overnight if necessary. Baste occasionally. Place dish uncovered in oven and cook for 45 minutes at 375°F (190°C) Gas Mark 5 until chicken is crispy golden.

Cook's Tip: You can use marmalade instead of redcurrant jelly.

Terence
Cuneo

MARINATED CHICKEN

This, of course, is one of my more sophisticated efforts and only broke surface after harrowing lessons at the stove-side from my daughter Linda. I should add in my defence, however, that given the time *and* the inclination, I am now able to turn out reasonably presentable simple meals and marinated chicken stands to this day as one of my cordon bleu creations. To my knowledge no one has died from it!

Serves 4

4 chicken breasts

3 tsp ginger

2 cloves garlic

1 small pot plain yoghurt

1 small pot double cream

1 frozen tub orange juice

Mix ginger, garlic, yoghurt, cream and orange juice together. Place chicken breasts in dish and pour the mixture over the chicken. Cover the dish and place in fridge overnight. Cook next day at 350°F (180°C) Gas Mark 4 for 1¼ hours – then serve.

CHICKEN WOODCOTE

This wonderful poultry dish has a distinctive continental flavour and reminds me of balmy summer evenings spent in the South of France.

Serves 4

8 chicken thighs
3 tbsp olive oil
8 oz (225 g) button mushrooms
1 glass of white wine
1 small tin tomatoes
1 tbsp chopped parsley
1 garlic clove crushed
4 fl oz (125 ml) chicken stock
Salt and pepper

Saute the chicken in the olive oil until brown on both sides. Add the mushrooms and cook slowly together with the lid on, turning occasionally, for about 35 minutes.

When cooked, remove chicken and mushrooms to a fireproof dish to keep warm. Add the remaining ingredients to the pan, stir well allowing to cook rapidly and reduce liquid a little. Strain the sauce over the chicken and sprinkle with chopped parsley.

Serve with new potatoes and broccoli.

Sir Edward Heath

FOUR TIME CHICKEN

Richard
Johnson

This is a way of making a chicken go a l-o-o-ng way without doing a great deal of work. When I say "a chicken" I mean a real chicken – a free range chicken, not some poor creature that's never seen the light of day in its short and miserable life in the battery house. Yes, I know the free-range ones are more expensive but they taste better and since we're talking about one of them providing four meals plus, I think the extra expense is worth it. If you don't agree, then that's all right too!

Serves 2

Meal 1:
CHICKEN CASSEROLED WITH SWEETCORN AND PEAS

1 chicken
2 medium onions
2 cloves garlic
1 tbsp butter
2 tbsp extra virgin olive oil
8 fl oz (250 ml) chicken stock or stock cubes
Small bunch of mixed fresh herbs or 1 tsp mixed dried herbs
6 oz (150 g) packet frozen mixed sweetcorn and peas
1 tbsp red or white wine, optional

Cut the chicken into serving pieces, remove skin and put it in a plastic bag with the carcase and the giblets and keep in fridge. I know this sounds a bit of a job, but it's really very simple to cut up the chicken and much better than buying pieces from the supermarket because you get the bonus of the carcase which is going to come in very handy later.

Skin the onions and garlic, chop them finely.

Heat the oil and butter in a heavy based flameproof casserole, the bigger the better, put in the chicken pieces and brown them on all sides – keep them moving so they don't stick to the bottom. Remove the pieces with a slotted spoon and set aside in a dish.

Cook the onion in the oil and butter mixture until it is soft, then add the garlic for a minute or two.

Stir in the chicken stock and add the herbs and wine. If you don't have any chicken stock, use chicken cube made up with water. Use salt free ones if you can find them. Too much salt is not good for the heart.

Add the chicken pieces and juices in the dish, cover and simmer over a low heat for 45 minutes, turning the pieces at half time. Add the defrosted sweetcorn and peas and cook for another 10 minutes.

When ready to serve, lift out as many pieces as you want to eat, spoon some of the corn and peas and some of the juice on to the plate and turn off the heat. If you've boiled a few potatoes while the casserole is cooking, so much the better. Leave the casserole where it stands, we'll deal with it tomorrow!

NEXT DAY:

Look into the casserole, you will see that the chicken pieces you didn't eat last night are embedded in a rich, jellified sauce. Resist eating the whole lot for breakfast! Take out the chicken and cut all the meat from the bones and reserve it. Toss the bones back into the casserole, add a few carrots, another onion and a couple of stalks of celery, roughly cut up. These vegetables will improve the taste of meals 3 and 4. Get the plastic bag out of the fridge and put the carcase and the bits of skin etc. into the casserole as well. Fill the casserole up to within a couple of inches of the top with fresh, cold water, chuck in a stock cube, if you have one, and set the heat to simmer the pot. Now for some lunch:

Meal 2:
CHICKEN SALAD WITH SWEET CURRIED SAUCE

5 oz (125 g) plain active yoghurt
1 tbsp extra virgin olive oil
1 tbsp curry powder
1 tsp sugar
1 tbsp pineapple juice or orange juice
Fresh grated black pepper
Cooked chicken meat, as above
1 clove garlic, crushed
1 tbsp lemon juice
1 tbsp fruit chutney
Pinch cayenne pepper
Chopped parsley
Mixed salad

Dice the chicken meat and stir all but about 2 oz of it into the curry sauce. Chill until you are ready to eat. Put the reserved chicken in the fridge.

Prepare a mixed salad. Place curried chicken mixture in the centre of each plate and scatter some chopped parsley on top.

Serve with some nice wholemeal bread or toast and butter. If you are like me, you might want a long cool glass of bitter beer too.

AFTER LUNCH:

You'll probably remember the soup and decide it's cooked long enough. Strain the liquid into a large bowl and set aside to cool. There should be several pints of the broth. Now for the 'plus' I mentioned above. If you keep a cat and dog, these people are in for a treat! Pick all the bits of meat and skin and veg out of the stuff remaining in the strainer. Mash all together, in the food processor if you have one. The pussy cat now has meals for several days, the hound, depending on size, will probably wolf it down in one sitting. When the broth has cooled completely, skim off all the fat from the surface, discard it. Keep the broth in the fridge.

MEAL 3:
HEARTY LENTIL SOUP WITH CHEESE CROUTONS

8 oz (225 g) orange split lentils
1 onion
2 sticks celery
1 tbsp extra virgin olive oil
8 oz (225 g) tin tomatoes
1 bay leaf
1 tbsp fresh parsley, chopped
1 large carrot
1 clove garlic
1 tsp dried mixed herbs
2 tsp ground cumin
1 vegetable stock cube
2 pints (1¼ litre) chicken stock

Opposite:
Dame Cicely
Saunders' Chicken
Pilaff

Croutons

2 slices of wholemeal bread

A little olive oil

1 oz (25 g) Parmesan cheese or old cheddar cheese, grated

Chop the onion, carrot, celery, garlic. Heat oil in large pan or casserole pot, add the vegetables and stir fry until they are tender.

Stir in tinned tomatoes, herbs, bay leaf, cumin, parsley and crumbled stock cube. Pour in chicken stock and add lentils. Bring to boil and immediately reduce heat – simmer for 45 minutes or until lentils are tender, but not mushy.

Meanwhile, cut some cubes of bread and fry them in a little olive oil, remove with slotted spoon, drain on kitchen paper and keep warm.

Serve the soup very hot and pass the croutons and cheese separately. If you don't feel like making the croutons, put a dollop of yoghurt into each plateful of soup and scatter some parsley on top. Some hot, garlicy bread from the oven and a glass of wine make this a luxury meal. You can buy garlic bread ready prepared.

MEAL 4:
CHICKEN SOUP WITH BAKED POTATOES AND SALAD

2 pints (1¼ litre) of chicken stock

2 baking potatoes, scrubbed and pricked

Handful of sour cream (for the potatoes)

Mixed salad

Take the stock and chicken meat from the fridge to make the soup. Bake the potatoes in the oven for an hour or until soft. Make up the salad from whatever you have left. An easy lunch!

I hope you will agree that our free-ranger, I hope it was, has done sterling service and provided good value for money. Well, anyway, whether you do or you don't, the cat and the dog are probably looking at you right now and hoping you'll get another one soon!

Opposite:
Derek Jameson's
Hot Tip

MEAT AND STEWS

LAMB FILLET CASSEROLE

Lady
Georgina
Coleridge

Serves 4

| 4 lamb fillets |
| 1 onion, chopped |
| Herbs – bay leaf, parsley, thyme |
| Salt (add when the meat is cooked) |
| Pepper |
| Worcester sauce |
| Stock to cover meat during cooking |
| 1 dstsp plain flour (to make sauce) |

Remove fat from lamb and cut meat into small pieces. Fry onion until golden brown. Fry meat until brown on all sides in a heavy based frying pan. Place in casserole dish. Add herbs and stock and three shakes of Worcester sauce. Cook in oven at 350°F (180°C) Gas Mark 5 for half an hour then reduce heat to 275°F (140°C) Gas Mark 1 for 2 to 3 hours until meat is tender. Add salt to taste if desired. Use flour to thicken stock to make a sauce.

PORK IN ORANGE SAUCE

This is an easy and nourishing recipe to use when preparing a meal to share with a special friend.

Lady
Ricketts

Serves 3 to 4

1 pork tenderloin, about 12 oz (300 g)

1 small onion

1 oz (25 g) butter or cooking oil

Plain flour

½ – ¾ pint (300-450 ml) chicken stock

½ large orange, finely grated rind and juice, a Seville orange in season is excellent

Salt and pepper

Melt butter or oil in frying pan and grate the onion into it. Add meat cut across the grain into slices of ⅓ inch thick, and brown on both sides. Remove meat to casserole, seasoning each layer with a little salt and pepper. Sprinkle enough flour into the pan to take the remaining fat, scraping the pan well.

Gradually add the stock, stirring until smooth and slightly thickened. Add orange rind and juice and pour over meat, bring to simmering point and cook in low oven 325°F (160°C) Gas Mark 3 for about ¾ hour until tender. Taste sauce and adjust seasoning.

This may be cooked on top of the stove provided it is just simmered and stirred occasionally to prevent sticking. It should then take about 30 minutes.

DEREK'S HOT TIP

Derek
Jameson

I call this recipe Jameson's Hot Tip because it says everything about my love of food that is rich and spicy – and that goes for life too!

Serves 3 to 4

| 1 lb (450 g) lean minced beef |
| 1 medium onion |
| 1 x 14 oz (400 g) tin tomatoes |
| 1 x 14 oz (400 g) red kidney beans |
| 1 x 5 oz (120 g) sliced mushrooms |
| 1 rounded tsp Cayenne chilli pepper |
| 2 tsp mixed herbs |
| 2 oxo cubes |
| Gravy browning |

Brown mince on low heat in frying pan, then transfer meat to a saucepan and add enough boiling water to cover meat. Leave on heat to simmer. Finely chop and boil onion, add to meat. Heat tomatoes in frying pan, stir into meat and add oxo cubes, salt and chilli and mixed herbs. Stir well adding gravy browning until chilli is thick. Allow to simmer for at least 20 minutes, topping up with boiling water if necessary. Stir in kidney beans and mushrooms, simmer for another 10 minutes and serve.

Serving Suggestions: Tastes best with plain rice or baked potatoes.

MEATBALLS IN TOMATO SAUCE

This recipe is always a hit with guests and best of all, apart from being delicious, it is easy to make.

Marjorie Proops

Serves 4

1 lb (450 g) minced beef or lamb
4 oz (100 g) sausage meat
1 tsp mixed herbs
1 crushed clove garlic (optional)
1 tbsp fresh parsley
1 medium onion, finely chopped
1 egg, for binding
Salt and pepper

Tomato sauce

1 tin tomatoes
1 onion
½ pint (300 ml) beef stock
Tomato puree

Mix all the ingredients together. With floured hands, roll small amounts into walnut size balls. Flatten each ball and put onto floured board. Fry them quickly in hot oil and butter for a minute or two. Drain on kitchen paper and put into a casserole.

Make the tomato sauce using tinned tomatoes. Chop the tomatoes and pour them with the juice into a frying pan in which you have fried a chopped onion. Add a little tomato puree for richness and half a pint of beef stock, made with a cube. Let this bubble for a few moments and then pour into casserole. Place the lid on the casserole and put on middle shelf in oven on 325°F (160°C) Gas Mark 3 for about two and a half hours.

The beauty of this dish is that you can leave it for much longer on a very low heat. Serve meatballs on plain boiled fluffy rice.

Sir
Clement
Freud

HAMBURGERS

Inspired by a friend who sells Hamburgers in a Discotheque – I have a wide circle of friends – and complains about having to buy pre-shaped 2 oz mounds of Hamburger meat at 18p a go, I tasted his wares. They were Hamburgers in the loosest sense of the word.

I gave him the following recipe which cut the cost to just under half: 1 lb (450 g) lean pork, 4 oz (100 g) pork fat, 3 oz (75 g) rusk (untoasted crumbs turn mixtures sour sooner), 4 fl oz (125 ml) water, 1 egg. Mince the first three ingredients, add water and beaten egg, season with salt, coarse ground black pepper, a heavy pinch of mace and mix well. The resulting mass will compare favourably with the filling of most pork sausages.

LAMB CHOPS A LA NAVARIN

Hubert
Gregg

This was a recipe of my mothers and since 'nostalgia' is my middle name, I am drawn to it as one of the joys of yesterday.

Serves 2

4-6 thin cut lamb chops or cutlets
2 oz (50 g) seasoned flour
1 tbsp cooking oil or lard
2 tbsp tomato puree
1 pint (600 ml) stock
1 bouquet garni – parsley, thyme, bay leaf
2 carrots, sliced
2 turnips, sliced
2 potatoes, sliced
1 onion, sliced, (optional)

Fry chops in oil until nearly brown. Remove from pan. Coat chops well with flour, return to pan and brown well. Mix tomato puree with stock and pour over chops. Bring to boil, add bouquet garni and simmer for 1 hour.

Add sliced vegetables and simmer for a further 1 hour.

MOTHER'S INDIVIDUAL SUET PUDDINGS

Bernard
Cribbins

Serves 3

12 oz (300 g) suet pastry

8 oz (225 g) mince

Slice ox liver, finely chopped

Sliced onion (optional)

Lard

Salt and pepper

Water or stock

Divide pastry into three and roll out into squares. Divide mince and liver into each square and put a dab of lard on each lot of meat. Sprinkle with salt and pepper, damp the edges and pull the sides up to almost close each parcel, pour in about a desertspoon of water or stock, then seal the edges.

Wrap each pudding in greased foil or floured cloths, tie up securely and boil or steam. Turn them over after an hour and cook for a further hour.

Cook's Tip: You could put onions in as an alternative. These puddings reheat and freeze well.

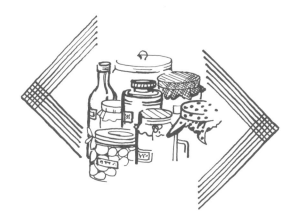

RABBIT STEW

**Sir Larry
Lamb**

For me rabbit stew is a gastronomic delight, full of flavour, texture and taste. For more than 40 years I have been privileged to eat in some of the world's finest restaurants and have yet to find it on their menus, so I include it here for you.

Serves 4

1 rabbit (2-2½ lb) ask your butcher to clean and joint it, retain liver and kidneys

4 oz (100 g) shin of beef, chopped

1 large onion, finely sliced

2 tbsp olive oil

4 oz (100 g) each swede, carrot, celery, potato

1 red pepper, de-seeded and finely sliced

1 pint (600 ml) chicken or beef stock

Dust rabbit joints, chopped beef and onion in seasoned flour. Heat oil in heavy based casserole with tight fitting lid. Cook the meat joints in hot oil for a few minutes, add all vegetables, coarsely chopped. Add chopped rabbit kidneys and liver. Stir well and season to taste. Cover with stock and bring to boil. Then simmer in slow oven 325°F (160°C) Gas Mark 3 for at least two hours.

Half an hour before serving skim and stir in ½ glass of cheap red wine; beer or stout can be used.

Serve with sliced green beans, al dente.

Cook's Tip: Rabbit freezes well if it has not been previously frozen.

NORTH COUNTRY LAMB AND BARLEY STEW

This stew is easy to prepare, nourishing and tastes good.

Dorothy Hollingsworth

Serves 2

Best end neck of lamb
2 oz (50 g) pearl barley
1 large onion
1 or 2 carrots
Salt and pepper
Water

Put the lamb into a casserole with chopped onion and carrots, pearl barley, salt and pepper. Cover with water, bring to the boil and skim. Simmer or cook in a slow oven 350°F (180°C) Gas Mark 4, until meat is tender, about 1½-2 hours.

SWEETBREADS HELENE

This recipe was given to me by Signor Leoni, Leoni's Quo Vadis Restaurant in Dean Street. Simply delicious.

Ellen Pollock

Serves 4

12 oz (300 g) calves sweetbreads
6 oz (150 g) white grapes
8 baby onions
8 oz (225 g) petit pois
Bunch of new carrots

Immerse sweetbreads in boiling salted water and leave to soak until all the skin is easily removed. Lightly fry.

Peel, pip and halve grapes. Place onions, sweetbreads and grapes in a casserole and bake for 1½ hours at 350°F (180°C) Gas Mark 4 on the middle shelf. Boil carrots and petit pois for 8-10 minutes. Serve all together on a large meat dish.

VEGETABLE AND BARLEY HOTPOT

The
Baroness
Thatcher

Serves 4

8 oz (225 g) pearl barley, soaked

6 oz (150 g) streaky bacon, rind removed, cut in squares

2 large onions, peeled and chopped

1 garlic clove, peeled and crushed

6 celery sticks, thinly sliced

2 medium courgelles, thinly sliced

12 oz (300 g) carrots, scraped and thinly sliced

8 oz (225 g) button mushrooms, sliced

1 pint (600 ml) chicken stock

3 tbsp chopped parsley

1 tbsp tomato puree

Salt and pepper

1 tbsp soy sauce

Cook the barley in boiling water for one hour and drain. Fry the bacon in a flameproof casserole over moderate heat until crisp. Remove with slotted spoon and set aside. Discard all but two tbsp of fat in the casserole.

Fry onion, garlic and celery for two minutes. Add courgettes, carrots and mushrooms. Pour on the stock and stir in the barley and bacon. Stir in two tablespoons of the parsley, tomato puree, salt and pepper and soy sauce and bring to the boil.

Cover the casserole and cook in a preheated oven at 350°F (180°C) Gas Mark 4 for 1 hour. Taste and adjust seasoning.

Sprinkle on remaining parsley and serve hot.

MEDITERRANEAN LENTIL STEW

Because this dish consists of pulses it is a good source of protein. Also it is a one-pot meal and therefore convenient and satisfying after a concert.

Serves 2

2 onions peeled and chopped
1 garlic clove, peeled and crushed
2 celery sticks, sliced
4 small courgettes, sliced
4 tomatoes, skinned and quartered
1½ pints (900 ml) water or stock
¼ tsp ground coriander
8 oz (225 g) brown lentils
2 tsp chopped parsley (optional)
Salt and pepper

Heat oil in large pan, add onions, garlic, celery and courgettes and fry gently for 10 minutes until lightly browned, stirring frequently. Add tomatoes, water or stock, coriander and salt and pepper to taste. Bring to boil. Add lentils, then cover and simmer for 1 to 1½ hours until the lentils are tender.

Alternatively, transfer ingredients to a casserole, cover and bake in a preheated moderate oven at 350°F (180°C) Gas Mark 4, for about 1½ hours.

Sprinkle with parsley and serve hot.

Sir Yehudi
Menuhin

PUDDINGS

APPLE CAKE

Sir John
Harvey-
Jones

As one gets older one is more interested in simplicity and quality. I believe this recipe represents both these virtues.

6 fl oz (175 ml) cooking oil
8 oz (225 g) castor sugar
2 eggs
Pinch of salt
2 tsp baking powder
1 tsp vanilla essence
8 oz (225 g) self raising flour
8 fl oz (250 ml) milk
3-4 eating apples or other fruit

Blend the oil and sugar together, add the eggs and beat. Add vanilla essence, baking powder and salt. Add the flour and milk alternately and beat. Pour into oiled baking tin.

You can now add 3 or 4 chopped eating apples to the mixture or you can substitute another fruit. Cook the cake in a medium oven 350°F (180°C) Gas Mark 4 for about 45 minutes.

This makes a very good dessert with cream.

Cook's Tip: The basic mixture can be adapted to include nuts, raisins, cherries, fresh fruit or coconut. Bran is also a good addition for extra fibre.

GUARD'S PUDDING

When we were children Guard's Pudding was always kept for very special occasions. It was on the menu for the lunch before my sister's wedding. It looks rather like a Christmas pudding so most of the guests chose fruit salad instead. This was good news for the family who knew how light it was in texture, and tucked into it with relish.

Brian Johnston

Serves 4

6 oz (150 g) fresh white breadcrumbs

6 oz (150 g) chopped suet or butter

4 oz (100 g) brown sugar

3 tbsp strawberry jam

1 large or 2 small eggs

1 level tsp bicarbonate of soda

Pinch of salt

Sauce

1 whole egg

1 egg yolk

1½ oz (40 g) castor sugar

2 large tbsp orange juice

Mix dry ingredients together. Add jam and egg beaten up with bicarbonate of soda. Mix thoroughly and then pour into a well greased mould which should be a little more than 3 parts full. Steam for three hours.

To prepare sauce, place ingredients in a bowl, and then stand the bowl in another bowl of very hot water. Whisk until thick and frothy. Serve immediately, or if not whisk for 1 minute before serving.

APPLE BROWN BETTY

Mrs Oliver
Lebus

Serves 4

4 slices bread, cut into small cubes

4 oz (100 g) butter, melted

6 oz (150 g) soft brown sugar

1 tsp cinnamon

Pinch of salt

4 large cooking apples, sliced

Mix bread cubes, butter, cinnamon, salt and sugar. Layer apple slices alternately with bread mixture in a 4 pint buttered baking dish. Bake for 1 hour at 375°F (190°C) Gas Mark 5 or until apples are tender and the top is golden.
   Serve with brandy butter or cream.

BANANA JAMAICAN

The
Countess
Mountbatten

This is a quick and easy dessert to prepare and also warming due to the small amount of rum.

Serves 2

2 bananas

½ miniature bottle of navy rum

1 tbsp dark brown sugar

Cream

Slice bananas lengthwise, then in half, place in a shallow oven-proof dish. Spoon over the sugar, then pour over the rum.
   Place in the oven at 400°F (200°C) Gas Mark 6 for 20-30 minutes, uncovered.
   Serve immediately with cream.

UPSIDE DOWN PUDDING

I chose this recipe because the name amuses me and I think the pudding must be a boon to many mothers of hungry children.

Jacquetta Hawkes

Topping

3 tbsp soft brown sugar

3 oz (75 g) butter

Pudding

2 oz (50 g) butter

5 oz (125 g) castor sugar

1 large egg

8 fl oz (250 ml) milk

9 oz (250 g) plain flour

4 level tsp baking powder

½ tsp salt

Stewed or canned fruit to cover base of pie dish

Cream topping ingredients and spread over base and side of tin. Arrange fruit on top.

Cream butter, add sugar and continue creaming and beat in egg. Sift flour with the baking powder and salt, fold into mixture alternately with the milk to dropping consistency. Turn into tin, on top of fruit, and bake for about 1 hour at 350°F (180°C) Gas Mark 4.

Turn out while hot, serve with custard or juices from fruit. Or allow to cool and serve as a cake.

Monica
Dickens

FRUIT FOOL

Serves 2

8 oz (225 g) fresh fruit – gooseberries, rhubarb, plums, etc.
or 1 tin fruit pie filling

1 small carton natural yoghurt, unsweetened

If using fresh fruit, stew it with very little water for about
15 minutes. Push through sieve, add sugar to taste. Whisk in
yoghurt.

DEVONSHIRE JUNKET

Eily
Blayney

It is an easily made 'treat' with little time required for
preparation – quite unlike the usual junket and really
delicious.

Serves 4

1 pint (600 ml) whole milk (not skimmed or semi-skimmed)

5 tbsp brandy

1 oz (25 g) castor sugar

1 tbsp rennet

¼ pint (150 ml) double cream

Cinammon mixed with sugar for decoration

3 tbsp milk

Warm milk and brandy to blood heat. Add sugar and stir in
rennet. Pour into serving bowl and leave until set but not in
the fridge. Whip cream with 3 tablespoons of milk and cover
junket. Sprinkle with cinammon sugar.

Cook's Tip: Instead of brandy you could use camp coffee or
strong instant coffee. The quantity of rennet should then be
slightly reduced. Rennet can be bought at Waitrose and
some chemists stock it. Store in the fridge.

Opposite:
Lord Rix's Mango
Fool *(front)* and Mrs
C P Fairbairn's Pussy
Pudding

HIGHLAND FRUITY

Follow this dessert with a sedate Scottish fling.

Serves 2

| 8 no-need-to-soak apricots |
| 8 no-need-to-soak prunes |
| 8 fl oz (250 ml) orange juice |
| 1 tbsp soft brown sugar |
| 1 tbsp whisky |
| 1 individual carton natural yoghurt |

Put apricots, stoned prunes, orange juice, and sugar into a food processor or blender and work until finely chopped and blended. Stir in whisky and yoghurt and spoon into individual dishes.

David
Langdon

PEACH DELIGHT

Because pensioners are 'peaches', well most of them!!! – and a delight.

| 1 tin sliced peaches in juice |
| Digestive biscuits |
| Whipping cream |

Drain juice from tin of peaches. Whip cream until stiff. Place two wedges of peach slices on a digestive biscuit forming a circle round the biscuit and leaving a gap in the middle. Put one teaspoon of cream on the centre of each biscuit.

Sir Cyril
Smith

Opposite:
Mary Whitehouse's
Melting Moments
(front) and Daisy
Hyams' Lemon and
Orange Cake

81

PUSSY'S PUDDING

Mrs C P
Fairbairn

Pussy's Pudding is easy to make with no cooking and can be as rich or not as you like. Cranachan is an old traditional Scottish recipe and again requires no cooking.

1 small carton whipping cream

1 small carton plain yoghurt

1 or 2 tins mixed fruit or fruit salad

Soft brown sugar

Whip cream until stiff and fold in yoghurt. If using mixed fruit chop first to bite size pieces and fold into cream mixture. Place in the fridge to cool and sprinkle with sugar before serving.

For a large party increase the quantities.

CRANACHAN

3-4 oz (75-100 g) oatmeal or 6 small oatcakes, well crushed

½ pint (300 ml) double cream

1 tbsp rum (optional)

4-6 oz (100-150 g) soft fruit, raspberries, blackberries, etc

Toast oatmeal or crushed oatcakes in a frying pan until lightly browned. Sift off any dusty meal and re-weigh oatmeal. Half whip double cream and add the rum. Fold in the oatmeal and then soft fruit – keeping a few berries back for decoration. Serve in glasses with fresh fruit on top.

Cook's Tip: There should not be too much oatmeal to cream.

MANGO FOOL

My wife and I always enjoy this dessert – it's quick and easy and foolproof!

Lord Rix

2 tins mangoes

½ pint (300 ml) double cream

Grated nutmeg

Strain mangoes and sieve. Whip cream and mix with mangoes. Sprinkle with nutmeg. Serve in individual dishes.

THE BYGRAVES SPECIAL

This is quick, easy to cook and the cost is minimal.

Max
Bygraves

Serves 4

1 pint (600 ml) double cream

1 large tin crushed pineapple

1 pineapple jelly

Strain all the juice from the tin of crushed pineapple. Cut up pineapple jelly.

Whip double cream. Pour pineapple juice into saucepan making the amount up to 1 pint with added water. Bring to the boil. Place the jelly cubes into a jug, pour over hot liquid and stir until dissolved. Allow to cool but not set.

Place whipped cream in glass bowl and fold in crushed pineapple. Gently pour over the very cool jelly. You will notice that the cream will rise in attractive shapes.

Allow to set in fridge for at least 2 hours.

CHOCOLATE POTS

Katie
Boyle

Everyone gets a little depressed from time to time and there is nothing more comforting, as you get older, than chocolate. By the time one has reached this stage in one's life, one doesn't worry so much about one's outline.

Serves 2-3

3 eggs, separated

6 oz (150 g) plain chocolate (grate a bar or use powdered kind)

2 tbsp cream

Whip the egg whites until stiff. Melt the chocolate and cream by putting both in a bowl and standing this in a pan of hot water on the stove. Then remove from heat, beat in egg yolks, fold in whites. Pour into individual dishes and chill. You can serve them with whipped cream on top.

Cook's Tip: This chocolate dish will keep for days in the fridge.

PEASANT GIRL IN A VEIL

Ann
Jellicoe

Serves 2

4 cooking apples

4 tbsp sugar (or to taste)

1 small carton whipping cream

Topping

2 tbsp breadcrumbs fried in a little butter *or*

2 tbsp Ovaltine granules

Peel, core and slice apples, add the sugar and stew them very gently using as little water as possible. Let the apples cool and then put them in a pretty dish. When quite cold whip the cream and spread over the apple. Fry the breadcrumbs and sprinkle over the cream. Alternatively, sprinkle over the Ovaltine which is lazy but no less delicious.

CHOCOLATE MOUSSE

This is very easy to make and requires no cooking, except to melt the chocolate, so could be prepared in a tiny kitchen or on a gas ring.

Dame
Margot
Smith

Serves 2-4

4 oz (100 g) plain chocolate
4 eggs
1 tbsp hot water
Vanilla essence
½ oz (12 g) butter
1 tbsp brandy
Whipped cream

Cut up chocolate and melt it in a basin over hot water. Separate eggs, beat yolks and add one at a time to chocolate, beating well. Add hot water and vanilla essence.

Cut butter into small pieces and add them one at a time, beating well. Add brandy and allow to cool. Whisk egg whites until very stiff. Fold into mixture with metal spoon and fold until all white disappears. Allow to set for at least 3 hours or overnight. Decorate with whipped cream and grated chocolate.

Needs no cooking and it is done very easily with electric beater.

Lady
Greenhill

ROSY APPLES CHARLISH

This is a very good rice and apple dish, nutritious and capable of infinite variations.

Serves 2

12 fl oz (350 ml) milk
1 rounded tbsp pudding rice
½ oz (12 g) butter
Pinch of salt
Little lemon rind or a bay leaf (optional)
1 heaped dstsp sugar
2 cooking apples
Raspberry or strawberry jam

Simmer all the ingredients except apples, jam and sugar in a double saucepan or a non-stick pan, until most of the milk is absorbed and the rice becomes tender. Stir from time to time. Then remove bay leaf or lemon rind if used and add sugar.

Peel and core the apples and roll in lemon juice. Place in a buttered fireproof dish and fill the core cavities with raspberry or strawberry jam, then fill the spaces around the apples with cooked rice. Bake in the oven 350°F (180°C) Gas Mark 4, for about an hour until apples are tender but not broken.

TEA-TIME

CARROT CAKE

Sir Freddie
Laker

6 oz (150 g) self raising flour

½ tsp bicarbonate or baking soda

½ tsp ground cinnamon

½ tsp ground cloves

8 oz (225 g) brown sugar

4 medium carrots, grated

3 oz (75 g) raisins or sultanas

½ tsp ground ginger

2 oz (50 g) chopped walnuts or almonds

¼ pint (150 ml) oil

2 eggs lightly beaten

Frosting

2 oz (50 g) cream cheese

1 oz (25 g) soft butter

1 tsp grated lemon rind

12 oz (300 g) icing sugar

Grease a loaf tin (14 cm x 25 cm), line base with greaseproof paper, then grease paper. Sift flour, soda and spices into bowl, stir in sugar, nuts, carrots, raisins and ginger. Finally stir in oil and beaten eggs. Beat on medium speed with mixer for 5 minutes. Pour into prepared tin, bake in oven at 350°F (180°C) Gas Mark 4 for about 1 hour. Leave the cake to rest for 5 minutes before turning onto a wire rack to cool.

To make the frosting beat together cream cheese, butter and lemon rind and gradually icing sugar. When the cake is cold spread the top with frosting.

This is a very moist cake.

NO COOK CHOCOLATE CAKE

The
Baroness
Serota

This is quick, easy and very popular with my family.

8 oz (225 g) digestive biscuits
4 oz (100 g) soft brown sugar
4 oz (100 g) butter or margarine
2 oz (50 g) raisins (optional)
3 tbsp cocoa
Little rum or brandy (optional)
1 egg, beaten

Melt butter and sugar gently in a pan, add raisins, brandy and cocoa. Remove from heat and add egg and coarsely chopped biscuits. Turn into greased 7" dish and chill in the fridge.

SWEET BISCUITS

Lady
Georgina
Coleridge

4 oz (100 g) plain flour
2 oz (50 g) granulated sugar
2 oz (50 g) softened butter
Pinch of salt
1 tsp vanilla essence
Little water

Mix flour, sugar and salt and then rub butter into the flour with fingertips to make a paste. Add vanilla essence and a little water and knead into a softish dough.

Roll out thinly, to an ⅛ of an inch. Cut into fingers and place on greased baking tray. Cook at 325°F (160°C) Gas Mark 3 for about 20 minutes. Watch they do not burn.

Cool on a wire tray. Very good with ice cream, fruit salad, etc.

MADEIRA CAKE

My father, who was a very skilled Scottish baker and confectioner, serving his time in perhaps one of the best bakeries in Edinburgh and at it for almost the whole of his life, certainly thirty-two years, was wonderful in all departments of the baking trade, but one of his specialities was the tea-time cake, and his madeira cake was second to none. A beautiful golden colour and a lovely buttery, eggy flavour with a crisp exterior that I shall never forget. I only wish I had taken the trouble to learn more from him and of his skills. Hope you find the cake as mouthwatering as I do.

Ronnie
Corbett

3 oz (75 g) butter
5 oz (125 g) margarine
10 oz (250 g) sugar
1 oz (25 g) glycerine
5 eggs
8 oz (225 g) cake flour
2 oz (50 g) self raising flour
Vanilla essence
2 tbsp lemon juice

Cream butter, margarine, sugar and glycerine until light and fluffy. Add half ounce of vanilla essence and lemon juice. Beat eggs, and add gradually to butter mixture.

Sieve flour and mix into batter. Set oven to 375°F (190°C) Gas Mark 5. Divide mixture into separate well-greased cake tins. Cook approximately 1 hour until risen, turn out on to wire racks and cool. Sprinkle with sugar.

This makes two good sized cakes.

COLD TEA LOAF

Daisy
Hyams

8 fl oz (250 ml) strong cold tea

4 oz (100 g) soft dark brown sugar

8 oz (225 g) mixed fruit

2 oz (50 g) candied peel

2 oz (50 g) cherries

8 oz (225 g) self raising flour

1 egg

Soak fruit and sugar in the cold tea. Leave to soak overnight.
Next day – add flour and beaten egg.
Bake for 1¼ hours at 325°F (160°C) Gas Mark 3.

LEMON OR ORANGE CAKE

5 oz (125 g) self raising flour

5 oz (125 g) soft margarine

5 oz (125 g) castor sugar

2 eggs

3 tbsp milk

1 large lemon or orange

3 tbsp icing sugar

Put all the ingredients, except orange, lemon and icing
sugar, into a mixing bowl and blend. Put into a loaf tin and
place in cold oven at 350°F (180°C) Gas Mark 4 for 50
minutes. Squeeze juice from lemon or orange and mix with
three tablespoons of icing sugar.

Prick cake when cold with fork and pour juice over it.

COCONUT ROCKS

This is quick, cheap, easy and extremely delicious!!!

Sir Harry
Secombe

4 oz (100 g) plain flour
4 oz (100 g) desiccated coconut
4 oz (100 g) butter
1 tsp baking powder
4 oz (100 g) ground rice
1 egg
6 oz (150 g) castor sugar

Cream the butter and beat in the sugar. Stir in the flour sifted with baking powder. Then add coconut and rice. Moisten with the beaten egg. Put out in little heaps like small rocks on a buttered baking tray.

Bake in a hot oven at 425°F (220°C) Gas Mark 7 for 15 minutes.

SHORTCAKE

One of my favourite and simple recipes which is served at meetings of the Harveys Leeds International Piano Competition.

Fanny
Waterman

6 oz (150 g) butter
3 oz (75 g) castor sugar
6 oz (150 g) plain flour
3 oz (75 g) cornflour

Beat the butter and sugar until light and creamy. Gradually add the cornflour and plain flour. Gently knead the mixture into a ball with cool hands. With finger tips and knuckles, press the mixture into an oblong tin until flat.

Lightly with a knife tip, mark the mixture into fingers. Using a fork, prick the top lightly all over. Bake in the middle of the oven at 350°F (180°C) Gas Mark 4, for 30-40 minutes until pale golden brown.

MERRIDALE MARY'S MELTING MOMENTS

Mary Whitehouse

We lived in Merridale Road in Wolverhampton and my children christened them!

1 tbsp syrup
1 tsp cooking chocolate
1 oz (25 g) margarine
2 oz (50 g) cornflakes

Heat syrup, margarine and chocolate until well mixed together. Take off heat and mix in enough cornflakes so that it all sticks together.

Spoon into individual paper cases and leave to cool.

LEMONADE

Dr Elizabeth Shore

3 lemons
1 lb (450 g) granulated sugar
1 pint (600 ml) boiling water
3 heaped tsp citric acid

Peel the lemons with a lemon peeler. Put peel into a jug with sugar. Pour on boiling water and stir with wooden spoon until sugar has dissolved. Leave to stand for 4 hours. Add juice of lemons and citric acid. Strain and keep in the fridge. Dilute with 4 parts water as a refreshing drink.

HERB JELLY

We have a large Bramley apple tree in our communal garden and as none of my fellow residents seem to eat apple pie or baked apples I decided to make a jelly with them, flavoured with herbs from my own little herb patch, which I hand around to friends as well as my neighbours.

Mary
Stott

Serve with either hot roast or cold meat, according to the nature of herbs used. Excellent way of using up windfalls.

Quantities according to apples available.

Either cooking or dessert apples can be used or a mixture of both. Wash the apples carefully but do not peel or core. Any bruised or damaged bits should be cut out and then the rest cut into pieces and put into a large pan with a mixture of three parts of cold water to one part of white vinegar sufficient to cover the apples. Add a large bunch of fresh mint and/or other garden herbs such us thyme, marjoram, hyssop, etc. Simmer together until the fruit is soft, then leave to drain overnight in a jelly bag.

Discard the pulp and measure the liquid. Heat it gently and gradually add 1 lb (450 g) of sugar to 1 pint (600 ml) of liquid. Test frequently for setting on a cold plate. It is ready when the liquid wrinkles when pushed with your finger nail.

Just before removing the jelly from the heat, add a few very finely chopped herbs and a few drops of green cooking liquid.

Skim before pouring into small, hot glass jars.

Keith
Waterhouse

KEITH WATERHOUSE

This is my only recipe:

YORKSHIRE PUDDING
(serves four)

Method

1. Ask spouse to make Yorkshire pudding

2. Repair to pub for two hours.

K.W.

INDEX